I0788955

This book belongs to

....

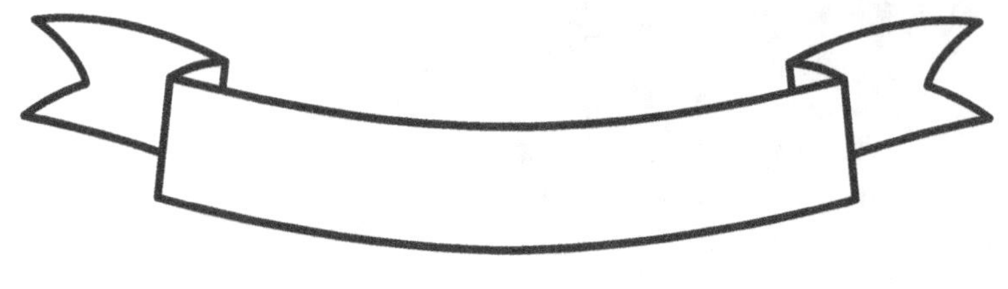

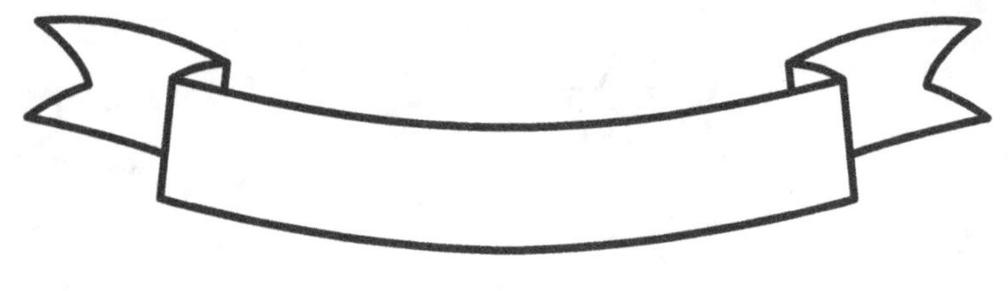

MILK
XOXO

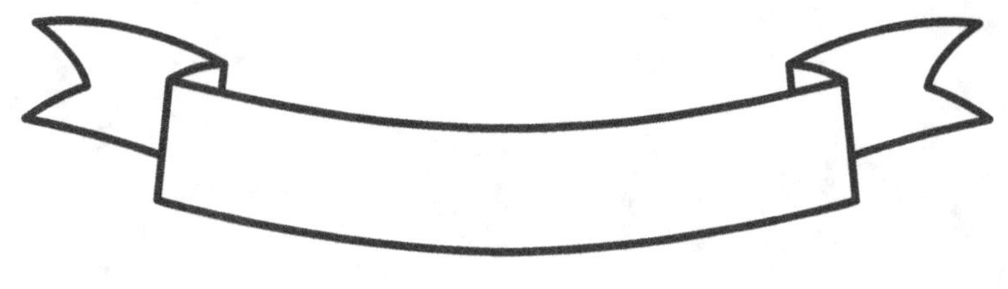

MILK
XOXO

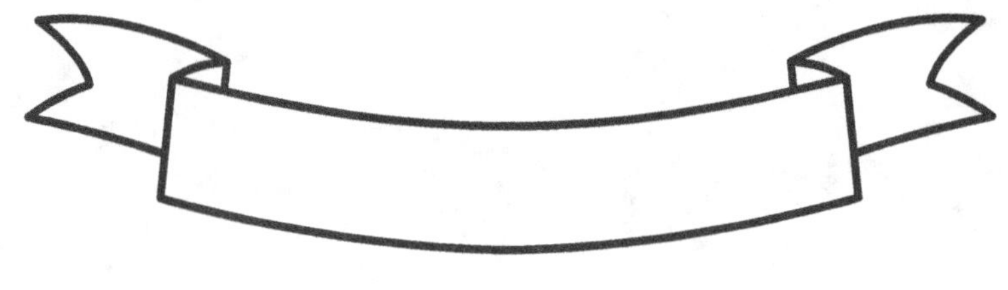

magic
Set 2

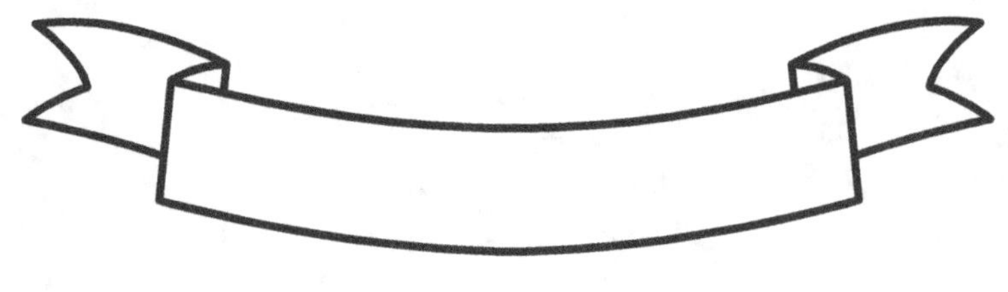

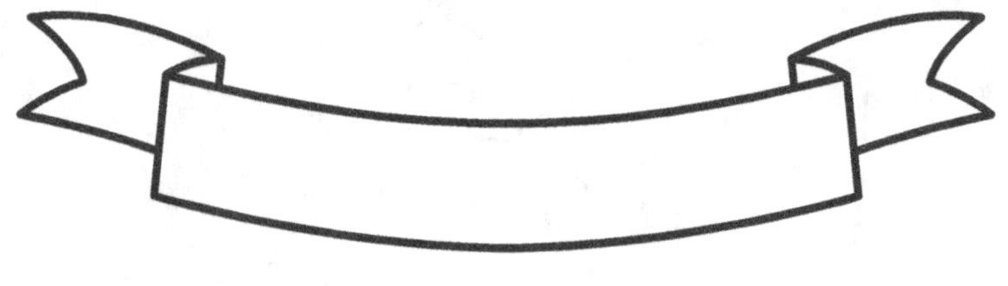

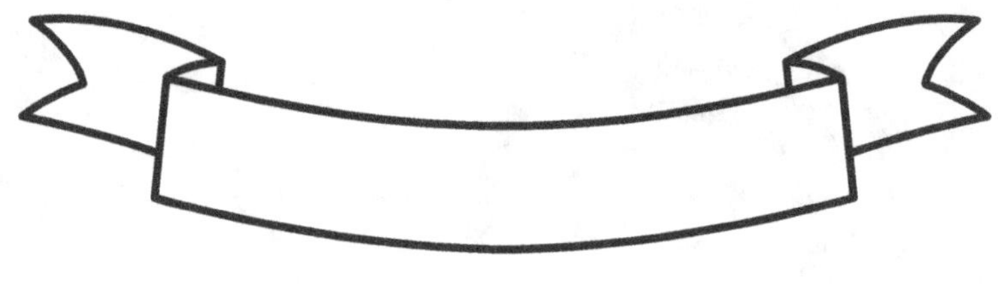

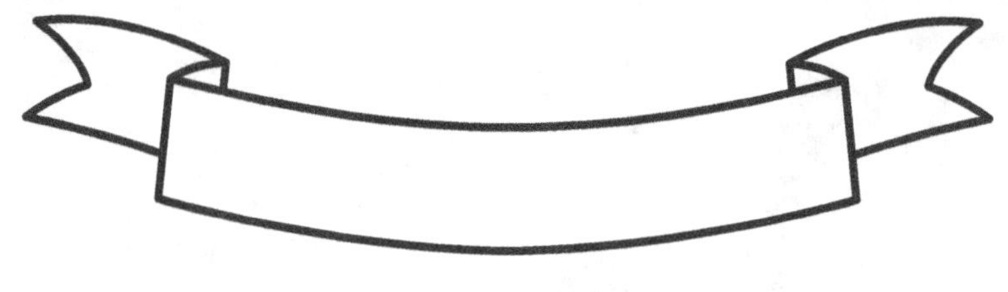

fairy tale

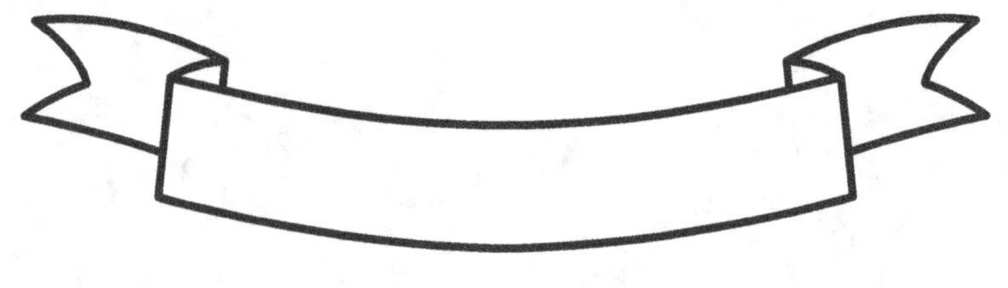

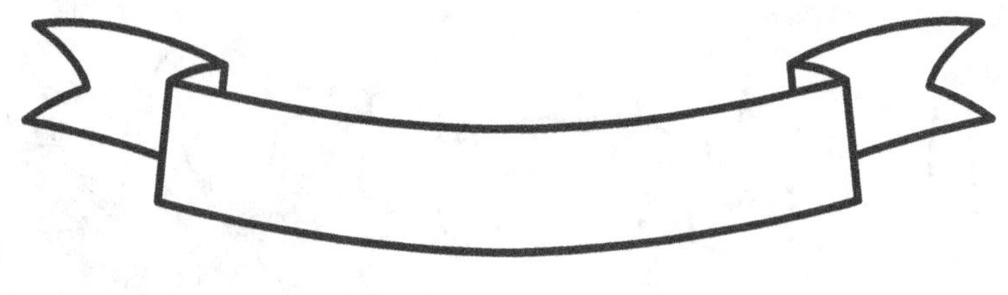

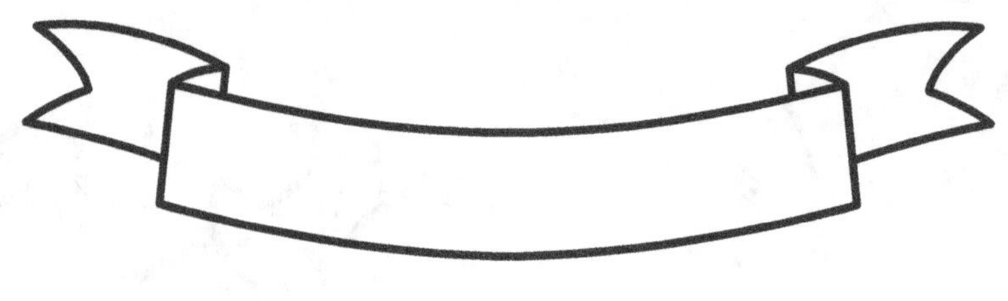

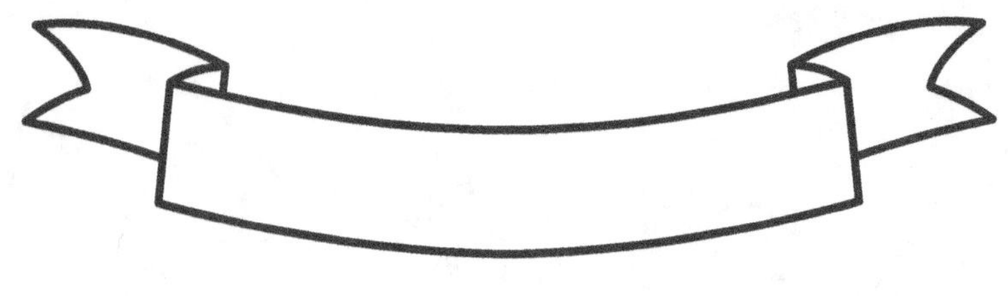

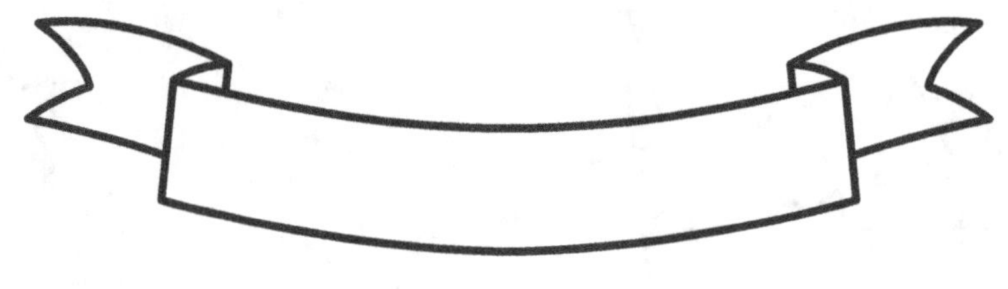

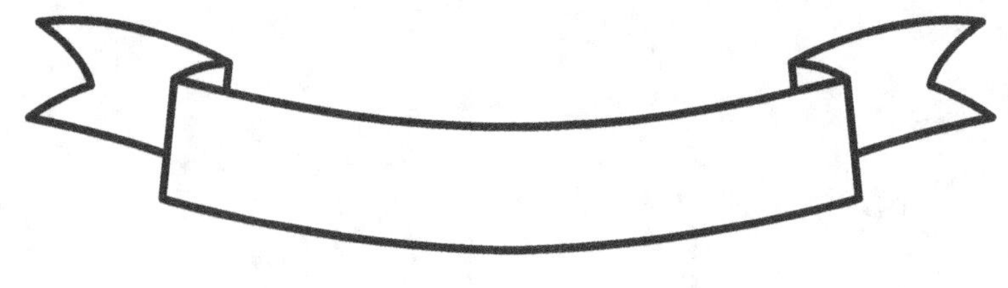

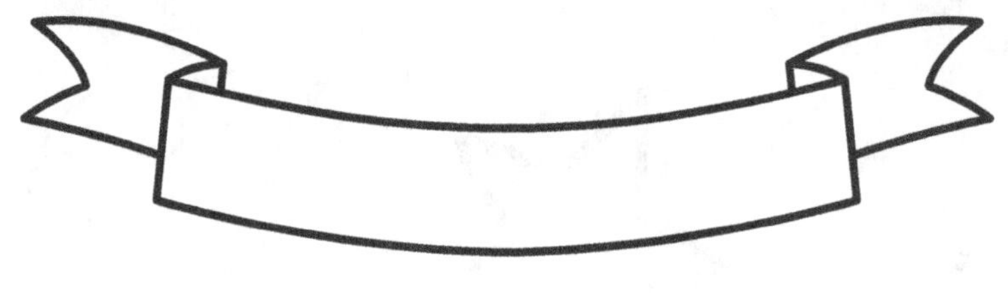

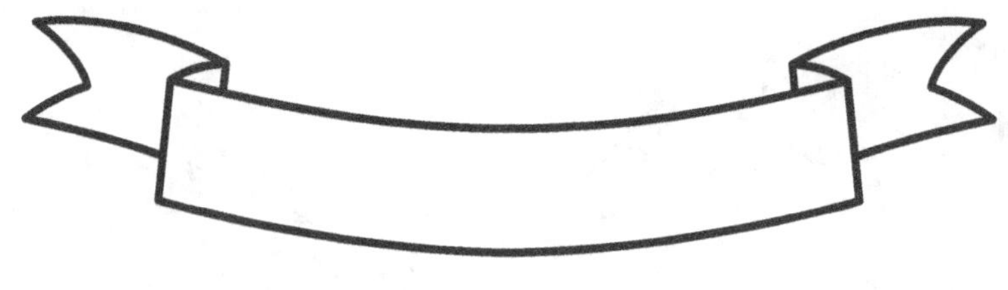

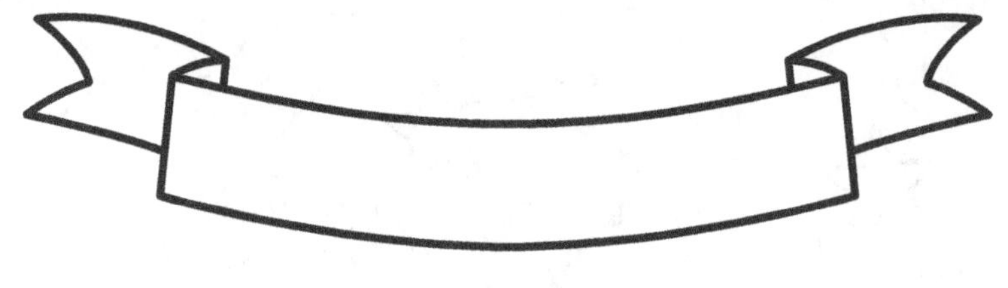

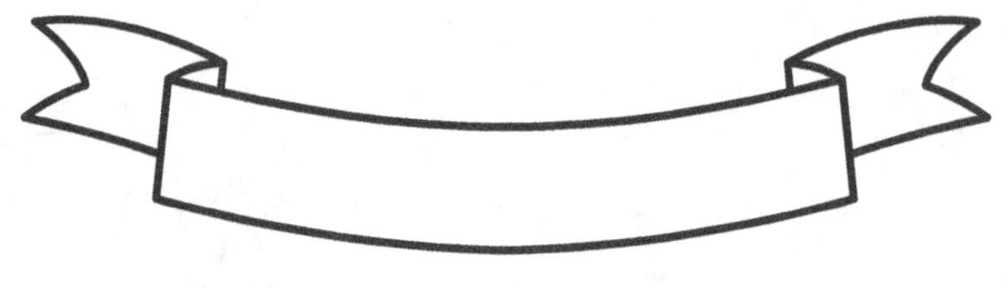

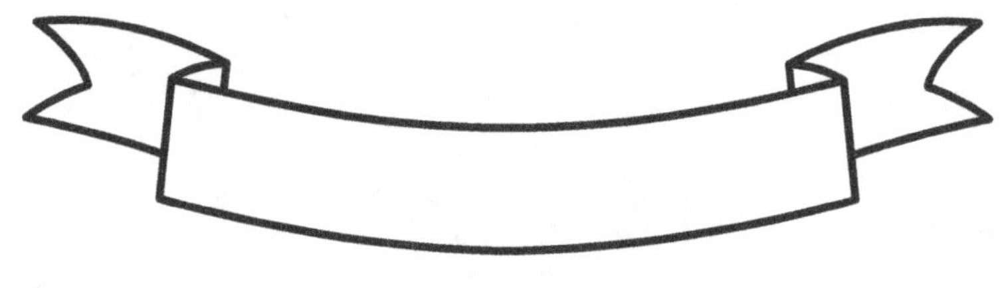

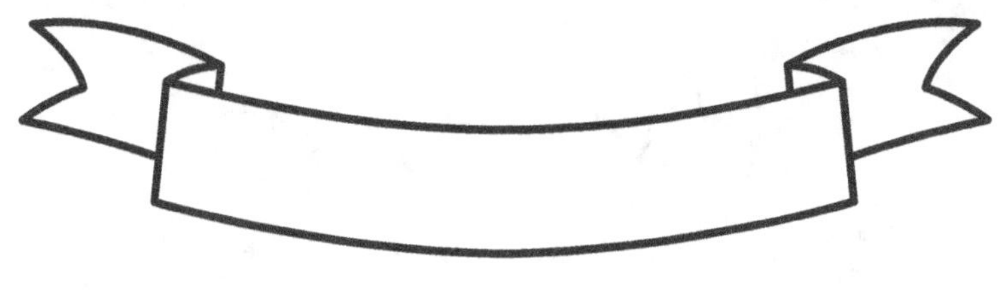 

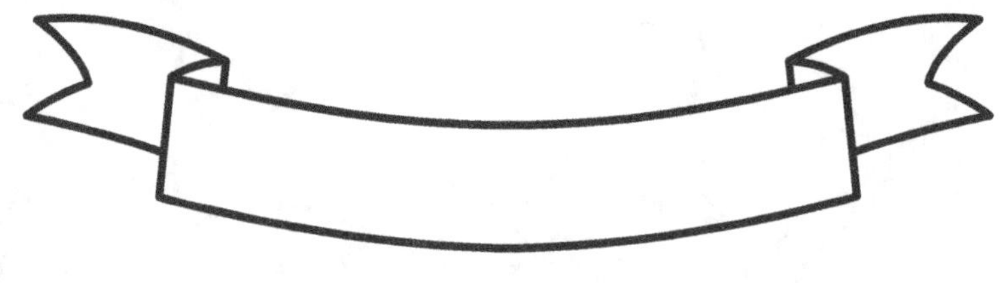

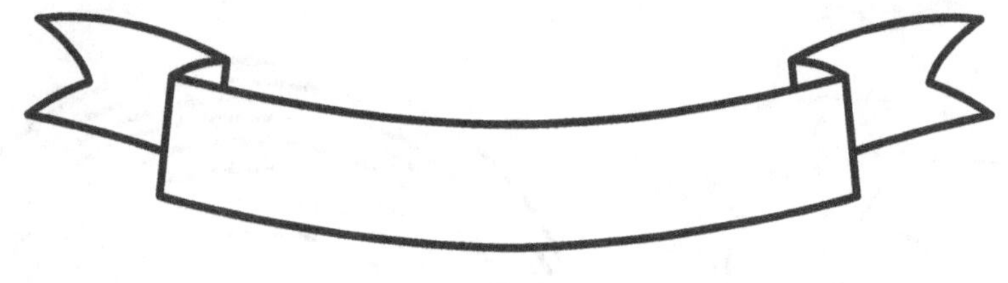

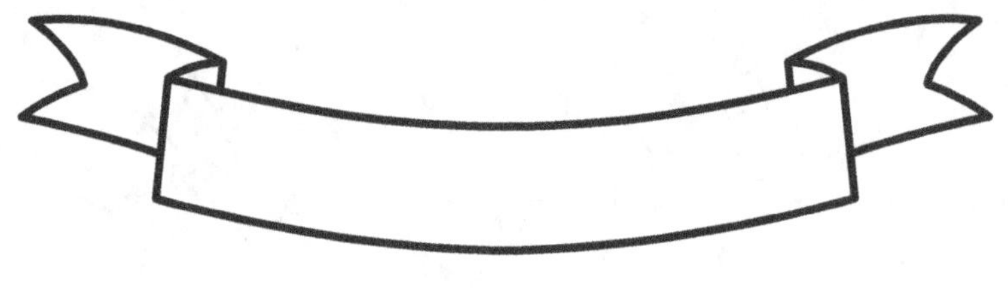

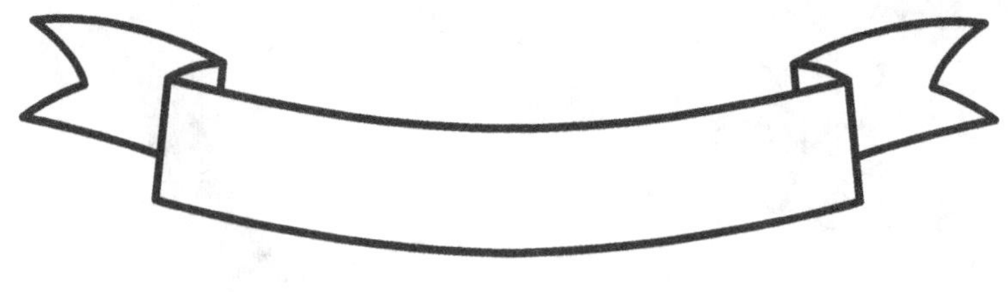

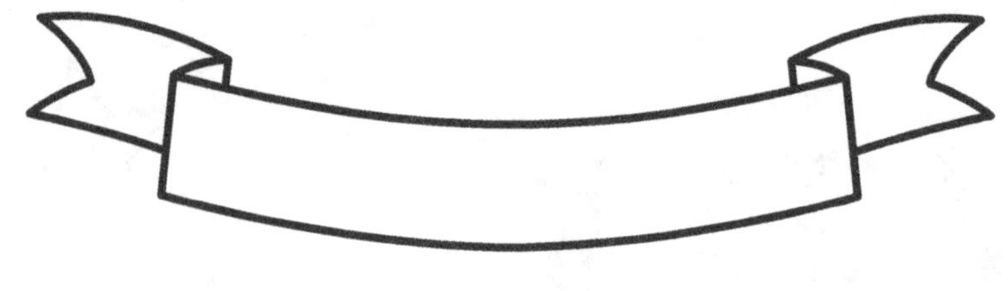

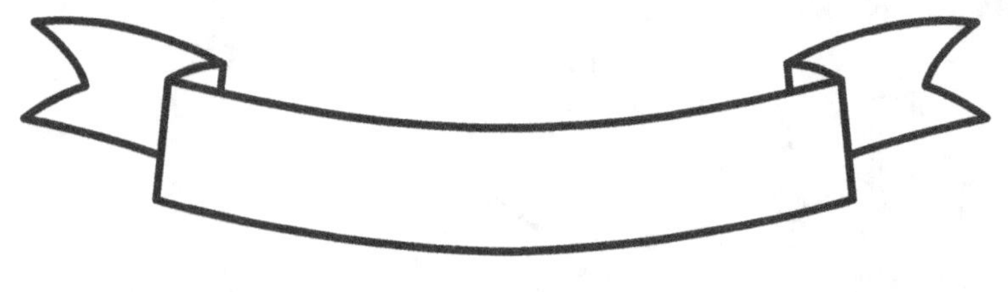

www.ingramcontent.com/pod-product-compliance
Lightning Source LLC
Chambersburg PA
CBHW080832260726

48654CB00026B/1440